Collins

Revised Edition

Vision 1

A Course on Values and Life Skills

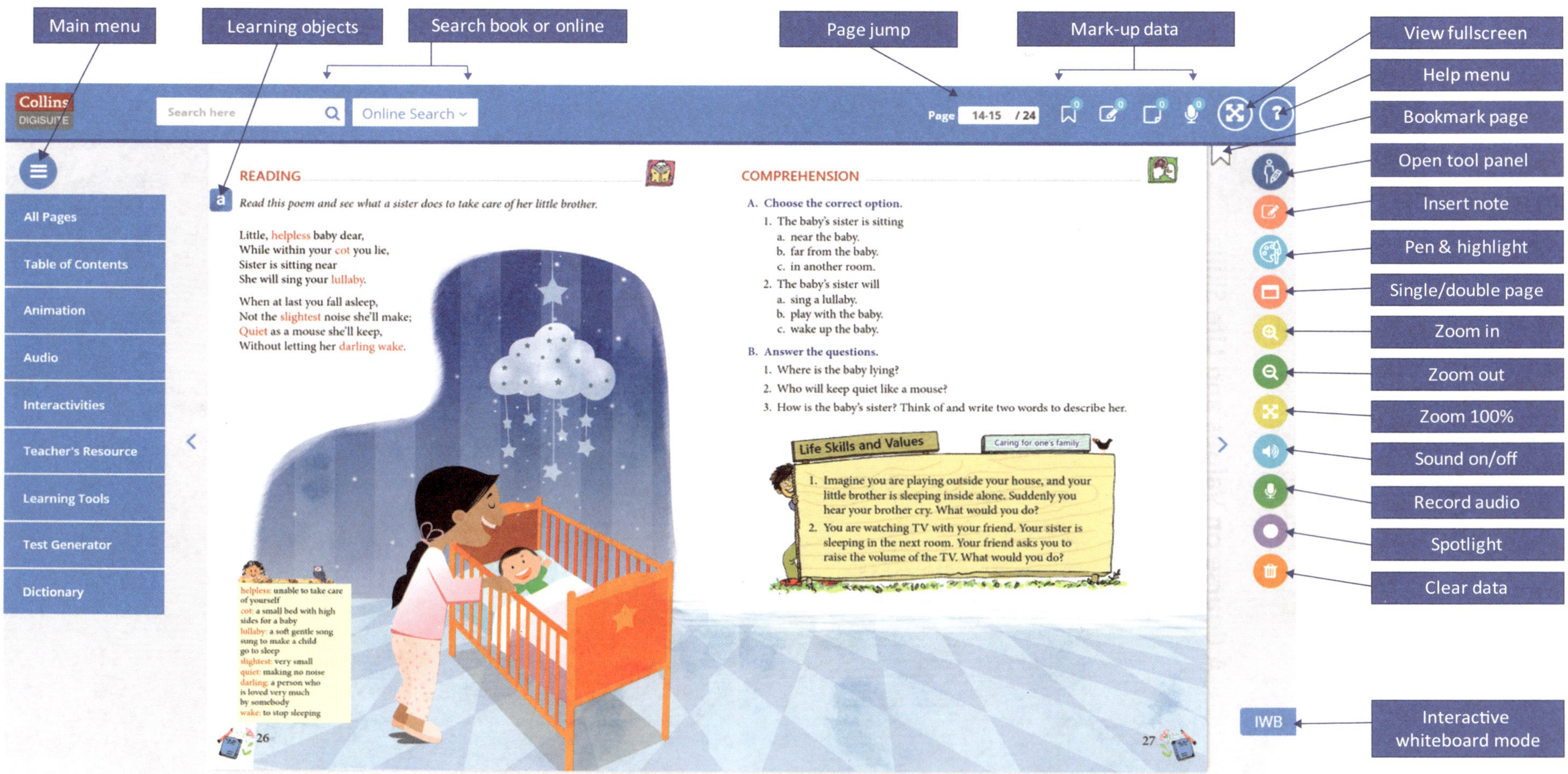

Main menu
Learning objects
Search book or online
Page jump
Mark-up data
View fullscreen
Help menu
Bookmark page
Open tool panel
Insert note
Pen & highlight
Single/double page
Zoom in
Zoom out
Zoom 100%
Sound on/off
Record audio
Spotlight
Clear data
Interactive whiteboard mode
Collins DIGISUITE
Search here
Online Search
Page 14-15 / 24
All Pages
Table of Contents
Animation
Audio
Interactivities
Teacher's Resource
Learning Tools
Test Generator
Dictionary
IWB
READING
a
Read this poem and see what a sister does to take care of her little brother.
Little, helpless baby dear,
While within your cot you lie,
Sister is sitting near
She will sing your lullaby.
When at last you fall asleep,
Not the slightest noise she'll make;
Quiet as a mouse she'll keep,
Without letting her darling wake.
helpless: unable to take care of yourself
cot: a small bed with high sides for a baby
lullaby: a soft gentle song sung to make a child go to sleep
slightest: very small
quiet: making no noise
darling: a person who is loved very much by somebody
wake: to stop sleeping
26
COMPREHENSION
A. Choose the correct option.
1. The baby's sister is sitting
a. near the baby.
b. far from the baby.
c. in another room.
2. The baby's sister will
a. sing a lullaby.
b. play with the baby.
c. wake up the baby.
B. Answer the questions.
1. Where is the baby lying?
2. Who will keep quiet like a mouse?
3. How is the baby's sister? Think of and write two words to describe her.
Life Skills and Values
Caring for one's family
1. Imagine you are playing outside your house, and your little brother is sleeping inside alone. Suddenly you hear your brother cry. What would you do?
2. You are watching TV with your friend. Your sister is sleeping in the next room. Your friend asks you to raise the volume of the TV. What would you do?
27

Preface

Vision Revised Edition, a course on life skills and values, is an engaging value education series meant to enable learners lead a balanced, happy and successful life. The National Education Policy, 2020 proposes the revision and revamping of all aspects of the education structure to create a new system that is aligned with the aspirational goals of 21st century education, while building upon India's traditions and value systems. It also lays focus on critical life skills and values.

Vision Revised Edition follows an interactive and multidisciplinary approach and caters to all kinds of learners with different learning styles.

Values are presented through progressively graded stories, anecdotes or poems.

Life Skills as laid down by the World Health Organization (WHO) have been covered through interesting stories.

Each book contains special chapters and colourful spreads showcasing the United Nations Sustainable Development Goals, which are important to achieve a just and an equitable world for all.

21st Century Skills have been mapped to each chapter with the aim of creating well-rounded individuals thriving in a constantly changing world.

Mental health and well-being of young learners is of prime importance in today's world. Therefore, Let's Do Yoga poster has been introduced as a brand-new feature of the book. It contains simple and doable asanas with step-by-step guidance and illustrations.

The series also focuses on mindfulness and social-emotional learning through 'happiness activities'. Young children learn by doing, hence the series has a variety of hands-on activities, encouraging quiet reflection and sound action.

Creating a safety net for children and making them aware of child rights is much needed in this age and time. *Vision* Revised Edition has special advice for children through which they can face situations in which they feel afraid, pressurized or unsafe.

Vision Revised Edition comes with Collins DigiSuite which offers digital content packed with animated stories, slideshows and interactive activities.

Vision Teacher's Manuals offer comprehensive Lesson Plans and Additional Worksheets for teachers.

In This Series ...

Vision Revised Edition adheres to the National Education Policy, 2020. Features such as 21st Century Skills, Life Skills, multiple intelligences, Sustainable Development Goals and Let's Do Yoga all align with the new policy.

Discuss

Warm-up exercise familiarizes students to the mood of the chapter

Read along

A story or a poem based on a value

Figure out

Questions based on the chapter to ensure value inculcation

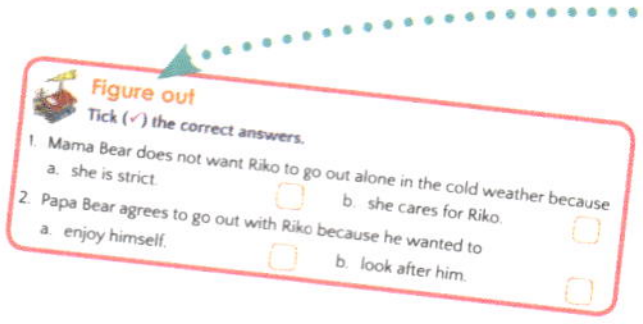

Relate

Application-based questions to check students' understanding

Project

Interesting projects based on the values taught

Happiness Activity

Interesting activities to promote 'happiness'

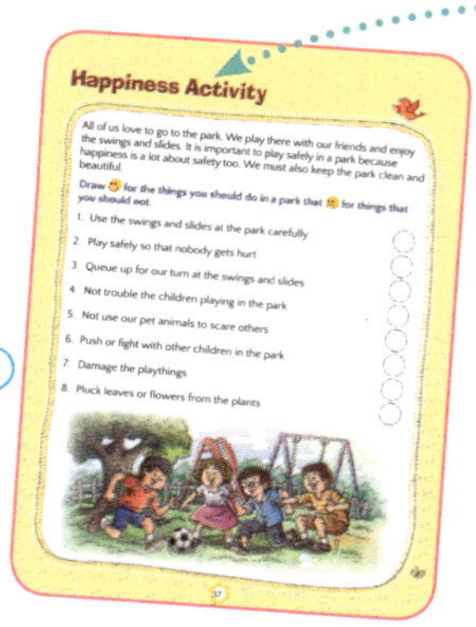

Remember

Brief pointers that the students can incorporate in their behaviour

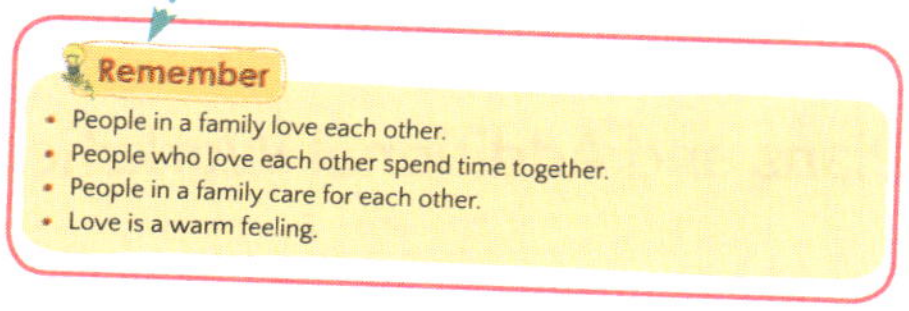

Think and Say

Thinking questions that encourage students to think laterally

Think and Say

When you come home wet on a rainy day, what do your parents do? Do you like that?

Happiness Box

Enjoyable activities that promote 'happiness' and exercises based on multiple intelligences addressing different learning styles

- Musical
- Interpersonal
- Visual-Spatial
- Verbal linguistic
- Naturalistic
- Intrapersonal
- Logical Mathematical
- Bodily Kinesthetic

Sustainable Development Goals

Special chapter and a colourful spread showcasing the UN Sustainable Development Goals, a set of goals aimed at changing our world for better

Poster

Colourful and interesting pull-out poster showcasing easy Yoga asanas

21st Century Skills

Skills necessary to succeed in the age of information: learning skills, literacy skills and social skills

Life Skills

Chapters focusing on WHO life skills through interesting stories

Teaching tips

- Talk about how strong determination helps the boy cross the stream.
- Tell children more stories about determination.

Teaching tips

Suggestions for teachers

Detailed Contents

21st Century Skills

Learning Skills	Collaboration	Riko's Day Out
	Critical Thinking	Buddy the Pup
	Communication	Kuki Learns the Rules
Literacy Skills	Information Literacy	Minnie at School
Social Skills	Flexibility	Bholu's Honey Bowl
	Initiative	Lola's Drawings
	Persistence	The Little Blue Engine

Life Skills

Babu and the Mango Tree A Good Deed	Empathy Creative Thinking

Projects

Project I Project II	Respect Nature Look Out!

Contents

1. Riko's Day Out

Discuss

Look at the pictures. Talk about them in class.

Read along

It is very cold outside. There is snow everywhere. Riko Bear wants to go outside and play. 'I cannot allow you to go out alone in this weather', says Mama Bear. Riko becomes sad.

Think and Say

When you come home wet on a rainy day, what do your parents do?

'Ok, Let us go together and have fun', says Papa Bear. Mama Bear wraps a muffler around Riko's neck and gives him gloves.

Riko and his father play in the snow. When they come back, they are shivering with cold.

'Come and sit down. Have some hot soup,' says Mama Bear with a smile.

Riko gives his mother a tight bear hug.

Remember

- People in a family love each other.
- People who love each other spend time together.
- People in a family care for each other.
- Love is a warm feeling.

Figure out

Tick (✓) the correct answers.

1. Mama Bear does not want Riko to go out alone in the cold weather because
   a. she is strict. ☐ b. she cares for Riko. ☐
2. Papa Bear agrees to go out with Riko because he wanted to
   a. enjoy himself. ☐ b. look after him. ☐
3. Mama Bear gives Riko a muffler and gloves because she is
   a. worried about him. ☐ b. angry with him. ☐
4. Mama Bear made hot soup for Papa Bear and Riko because she
   a. loves them. ☐ b. is unhappy they went out. ☐
5. Riko gives his mother a tight bear hug. It is his way of saying,
   a. 'I am sad'. ☐ b. 'Thank you'. ☐

Relate

Draw a 🙂 for the best answer.

1. Your grandfather wants your help to take his medicine. What would you do?

a. Continue playing ◯

b. Help him take his medicine ◯

2. Your mother helps you finish your homework. What would you do to thank her?

a. Hug her

b. Demand an ice cream

3. Your father comes home tired from office. What will you do to show your love?

a. Switch on the fan

b. Jump on the sofa

Happiness Box

1. Paste pictures of your family members having fun here.

2. **Look at the picture. The grandmother is reading a book to her granddaughter. Write about how you spend time with your grandparents.**

....

....

....

....

....

....

....

....

....

3. **Sing this poem to a melody.**

My mother has a sharp mind,
My father is gentle and kind.
My brother loves football,
My sister has grown so tall!
My grandfather is funny.
Grandmother's favourite weather is sunny
My uncle is so much fun,
My aunt has eyes as bright as the sun.
We all live happily,
I love my big family.

Teaching tips

- Give examples of parental care and talk about how students can show that same care and affection towards their elders.
- Stress on unselfishness.
- Stress that students should consider the comforts of others before their own.

2. Bholu's Honey Bowl

Discuss

Look at the pictures. Talk about them in class.

Read along

Bholu the Bear and Pinky the Rabbit are very good friends.

They play together. They run after butterflies together.

They take a dip in the river together. They share their food.

One day, Pinky goes to Bholu's house to play.

At the door, she hears Bholu's mother talking to him.

'Bholu, it's time for you to eat. Here is a bowl of honey', she says. 'You will have to make do with this small bowl. I am going to get some more from the market'.

Think and Say

What will you do if you have money to buy only one ice cream but your friend also wants one?

His mother gives him a small bowl of honey and says, 'Finish it by the time I am back from shopping'.

Pinky knocks on the door and enters.

'Hello Friend!' says Pinky.

'Hello Pinky! Come, share some honey with me', says Bholu.

Pinky is surprised.

'Bholu, this honey is so little. If I eat from your bowl, what will you have?' asks Pinky.

'We will share the honey

because you are my friend', replies Bholu.

'I love you, Bholu!' says Pinky.

Pinky and Bholu then finish the honey together.

Just then, Bholu's mother comes home and sees how much the friends love each other. She takes out the honey from her shopping bag and fills two bowls with it. She gives the bowls to the two friends.

Bholu and Pinky scrape the bowls clean, enjoying the honey.

—Sutapa Basu

Remember

- Share things with your friends.
- Enjoy your friends' special days.
- Play with your friends, even if they are different from you.
- Help your friends when they are in need.
- Do not hurt your friends.

Figure out

Tick (✓) the correct answers.

1. Bholu and Pinky do everything together because they are
   a. good friends. ☐ b. not friends. ☐
2. Pinky went to Bholu's house to
   a. have honey. ☐ b. play. ☐
3. Bholu offers to share his honey with Pinky because
   a. Pinky is his friend. ☐ b. Pinky likes honey. ☐

4. Pinky is surprised that
   a. Bholu wants to share the little honey he has. ☐
   b. Bholu's mother had gone to the market. ☐
5. Bholu's mother gives them two more bowls of honey because
   a. Bholu showed his love for his friend by sharing the honey. ☐
   b. Bholu asked for more. ☐

Relate

Draw a 🙂 for the best answer.

1. Your friend and you are playing at night and suddenly the lights go off. She is afraid of the dark. What would you do?

a. Try to scare her ○

b. Talk to her till the lights come back ○

2. One of your friends cannot walk easily. What would you do?

a. Play the games he can play ○

b. Not play with him ○

3. Your friend and you take part in a race. She wins but you do not. How will you behave?

a. Feel sad ○

b. Feel happy for your friend ○

Happiness Box

1. Make friendship bands and gift them to your friends.

1. Take a strip of paper and wrap it around your friend's wrist.
2. Stick the ends of the band with glue.
3. Decorate the band using colours.

2. Tick the things you will do to make your different friends feel special.

1. Show respect towards them. ☐
2. Not pay attention to their needs. ☐
3. Always offer them help. ☐
4. Spend time with them. ☐

3. How many children in the class are your friends?

Make two new friends in your class. Tell them your name, where you live and what you like to play. Then ask them to tell you something about themselves.

Teaching tips

- Explain the importance of sharing with siblings.
- Tell more stories about sharing and the happiness it brings.
- Talk about underprivileged children and the importance of sharing with them.

SDG 3 Sustainable Development Goals

3. I Want to Be Clean

Discuss

Look at the pictures. Talk about them in class.

Read along

Good health and well-being are important goals that the whole world is trying to achieve. People of all ages should try to be healthy. We should eat well and stay clean. We should encourage others to do this as well, just like little Karim's friends did.

Little Karim was spending his holidays with Grandmother. Every morning Grandmother dressed Karim in clean clothes and shiny shoes. Yet, Karim walked in with muddy shoes, a dirty T-shirt and a grubby face after coming from the playground.

Grandmother would say, 'Please wash your hands, Karim'.

Grandmother would say, 'Please take a bath, Karim'.

Grandmother would say, 'Please change into clean clothes, Karim'.

Karim would just hurriedly wash his hands and dust his clothes. He would not take a bath or change his clothes. He would sit down to eat.

Grandmother said, 'Karim, clean up before eating. Dirt brings germs. Germs will make you sick'.

Little Karim did not bother.

One afternoon, little Karim was in the garden playing with mud. Suddenly, he heard someone call, 'Rover! Rover! Walk behind me.'

Think and Say

Before you sit down to eat your meals, what should you do to keep healthy? After you eat your dinner and before you go to sleep, what should you do to keep healthy?

Karim peeped over the fence. His neighbour, Samrat, was walking with a beautiful white dog. The dog's fur was shining in the sunlight.

A bright red collar was on his neck. Its nails were trimmed, and it smelled of vanilla dog shampoo. Karim loved dogs.

The other children came out to see Samrat's dog. They wanted to pet Rover. Samrat said, 'Please do not touch Rover with dirty hands. Dirt brings germs and Rover will fall sick'.

Karim wanted to pet Rover, too. He looked at his hands and clothes. They were covered with mud.

Karim ran home. Grandmother was surprised to see him rushing to take a bath. Karim bathed and changed into clean clothes. He put on shining shoes. Then, he dashed out to meet Rover.

It was great fun playing with Rover. From that day onwards, little Karim never missed a bath in his life. He kept clean all day, too.

Remember

- Bathe every day and wear clean clothes.
- Wash your hands every time you come back home. Avoid touching your face with dirty hands.
- Carry a hand sanitizer with you. Use it whenever you touch any surfaces outside.
- Eat healthy food and wash your hands before and after meals.
- Cover your nose and mouth with a mask in crowded and polluted areas.

Figure out

Tick (✓) the correct answers.

1. Grandmother did not like dirt because
   a. it brought germs and sickness. ☐
   b. she had to clean it. ☐
2. Grandmother wanted Karim to be clean because
   a. it would keep him healthy. ☐
   b. his clothes would need to be washed. ☐
3. Karim did not clean himself because
   a. he did not want to bother with it. ☐
   b. he wanted to make the house dirty. ☐
4. Karim could not play with Rover because
   a. his muddy hands could make Rover sick. ☐
   b. he was afraid of Rover. ☐
5. Karim became a clean boy because
   a. he wanted to play with Rover. ☐
   b. there was no more mud to play with. ☐

6. Grandmother was surprised because
   a. Karim rushed to take a bath
   b. Karim ate healthy food

Relate

Draw a 🙂 for the best answer.

1. On a cold winter morning, which one of these will you do?

a. Bathe with warm water before going to school

b. Skip bathing before going to school

2. When you sweat in the heat, what do you wipe your face with?

a. With my hand

b. With a clean handkerchief

3. Which one of these should you do regularly?

a. Trim my nails

b. Let my nails grow long and dirty

Happiness Box

1. Many germs stick to our hands when we go out. Follow these steps to wash your hands properly.

2. Write three things you do to stay clean every day.

3. Join the things that match each other.

Teaching tips

- Stress on the fact that in the story it was the child's decision to clean up.
- Values are integrated only when children feel that they are means to a valuable end. Talk about values with the students, keeping this point in mind.

4. Buddy the Pup

Discuss

Look at the pictures. Talk about them in class.

Read along

Noni has many friends in school but they all live far away. When she is at home, she has no one to play with. Noni feels lonely.

One day, Noni says to her mother, 'Mother, I want a little puppy.'

'Why do you want a puppy?' asks her mother.

'I want a friend at home', replies little Noni.

In the evening, Noni's mother and father take her to a man who has lots of puppies. He is the owner of a kennel. A kennel is a place where dogs are kept and looked after.

Noni is happy to see so many cute, little puppies. Some of them are quarelling, some playing with each other and some are sitting.

'Take any one you like,' the kennel owner says.

The kennel owner shows her different puppies and tells her about them. 'See, this puppy is a naughty one.

That one has black fur and the other one there runs very fast', said the kennel owner, pointing to the different puppies.

Noni looks at the puppies. 'Why is that puppy sitting alone there?', she points to a puppy.

'Oh! This puppy? He has a short leg. He cannot run properly', explains the kennel owner.

'Is that the reason other puppies don't play with him?' asks Noni.

The kennel owner nods.

'Mom, Dad, I will take the puppy with the short leg', Noni says.

Surprised, the kennel owner asks, 'Why did you choose him?'

'As both of us are lonely, we can be each other's friend', says Noni. Mother and Father are happy with Noni's choice.

Think and Say
How can you look after the stray animals that live in your neighbourhood?

'You can protect him and care for him', says Mother.

'What will you call him?' asks Father.

Noni picks up the puppy and says, 'I'll call him Buddy'.

Remember

- Our pet animals can be our best friends.
- Show love, care and kindness towards animals.
- Give food and water to your pets.
- Animals and birds also feel pain, so never hurt them.

Figure out

Tick (✓) the correct answers.

1. Noni has many friends because she is
   a. a bully. ☐ b. friendly. ☐
2. Noni wants to have a puppy because she
   a. wants a friend. ☐ b. wants an animal. ☐
3. A kennel is a place where
   a. dogs are kept and bred. ☐ b. cats are kept and bred. ☐

4. The dogs did not play with the puppy with a short leg because
   a. he could not run well.
   b. he ran faster than the other puppies.

5. Noni chose the puppy with a short leg because
   a. he was lonely.
   b. she was afraid of the other puppies.

Relate

Draw a 🙂 for the best answer.

1. You find a beautiful butterfly inside your room. What would you do?

a. Try to catch it

b. Let it fly away

2. It is raining outside and a frog has entered your house. What would you do?

a. Try to hurt it

b. Let it go

3. Your kitten is playing with yarn. What would you do?

a. Gently take it away

b. Snatch it

Happiness Box

1. Make a birdbath and a bird feeder for your feathered friends. Here is how you can make it.

a. Take a clay or mud dish with a wide rim. Fill it with water. Keep it outside your house. This is called a birdbath.

b. Ask a few elders and find out what kind of grains birds like to eat.

c. Keep a few grains near the bird bath for the birds to feed on.

Enjoy watching the birds come to your house every day.

2. Draw your favourite pet here and write its name. Tell your class how you would take care of it.

Teaching tips

- Discuss how keeping pets makes us happy.
- Tell students that enjoying the company of pets also means caring for them and training them.
- We must care for stray animals too and not just for our pets.

5. Babu and the Mango Tree

Discuss

Look at the pictures. Talk about them in class.

Read along

Babu lives with his family in a small house with a huge garden in the town.

Behind Babu's house is a tall mango tree. Babu loves climbing the tree. He plays in its shade. He also eats mangoes from the tree.

Babu's grandfather wants to visit the family.

Babu's mother says, 'Babu, you will have to share your room with Grandpa'. Babu nods happily.

Father says, 'Babu, I am happy you like to share your room with Grandpa. Please remember, Grandpa is old. He needs to rest. Be careful not to make too much noise in your room'.

'Where will I play then?' asks Babu, worried.

Father and Mother thought for a while.

Then, Mother says, 'You do like the mango tree, right?'

'I love the mango tree. It gives me shade and mangoes', says Babu.

'You are right, Babu', says Mother, 'Do not worry, we will think of a place for you to play'.

Next day, Babu returns from school. He finds all his toys missing from his room.

'Where are my toys?' asks Babu.

Think and Say

Have you ever climbed a tree or sat under its shade? Did you feel happy doing so?

His mother takes him outside and points to the tree. There is a tree house on a big, thick branch of the tree.

'We made a special place for you', says Mother. 'You can play there with your friends. You can make as much noise as you like'. She smiles, 'Grandfather can rest in the room.'

'Yippee!' Babu says, running to the tree.

Babu loves playing in his tree house.

—Sutapa Basu

Remember

- We should respect the needs of others.
- We should adjust to the needs of our elders.
- Trees and plants are our friends.
- We get many important things from trees.

Figure out

Tick (✓) the correct answers.

1. Babu agrees to share his room with his grandfather because
   a. he respects his grandfather. ☐
   b. he is afraid of his grandfather. ☐
2. Father asks Babu
   a. not to make a lot of noise in his room. ☐
   b. to dance in his room. ☐
3. Mother shows Babu a room and says that it is his
   a. tree house. ☐
   b. school. ☐
4. Babu is happy because
   a. he has a new place where he can play as much as he wants. ☐
   b. the mango tree was not cut down. ☐
5. When Babu came back from school, he found that
   a. his parents had bought him a gift ☐
   b. all his toys were missing from his room ☐
6. Babu loved the mango tree because
   a. it gave him shade and mangoes ☐
   b. Babu's favourite bird lived on it ☐

7. Where does Babu live?

a. In a small house with huge garden

b. In a huge house with small garden

Relate

Draw a 🙂 for the best answer.

1. Your father asks you to water the plants in your garden every day. What would you do?

a. Not water the plants

b. Water the plants every day

2. You are playing with a ball and it rolls into a bed of flowers. What would you do?

a. Walk all over the flowers to get the ball

b. Look for the ball carefully without crushing the plants

3. Your family goes for a picnic in the woods. How would your cousins and you behave?

a. Pluck the flowers

b. Care for the plants

Happiness Box

1. Read this poem and act it out.

Little Brown Seeds

Little brown seeds
small and round.

Are you sleeping
under the ground?

Here comes the raindrops
Sprinkle, sprinkle, sprinkle.

High up shines a rainbow
Twinkle, twinkle, twinkle.

Little brown seeds
Wake up below.

Up through the earth they
Grow, grow, grow.

Little green leaves
Come one by one.

They hold up their heads
And look at the sun.

2. Time yourself and say the names of any ten flowers that you know. You should not take more than thirty seconds.

Teaching tips

- Stress on respecting elders.
- Talk about the importance of respecting and protecting nature.
- Talk about the little adjustments humans can make to live in harmony with nature and with people around us.

Happiness Activity

All of us love to go to the park. We play there with our friends and enjoy the swings and slides. It is important to play safely in a park because happiness is a lot about safety too. We must also keep the park clean and beautiful.

Draw 🙂 for the things you should do in a park that ☹️ for things that you should not.

1. Use the swings and slides at the park carefully ◯
2. Play safely so that nobody gets hurt ◯
3. Queue up for our turn at the swings and slides ◯
4. Not trouble the children playing in the park ◯
5. Not use our pet animals to scare others ◯
6. Push or fight with other children in the park ◯
7. Damage the playthings ◯
8. Pluck leaves or flowers from the plants ◯

Colour the picture. Circle the wrong actions.

Project I : Respect Nature

We know that trees are our friends. They keep our surroundings cool and clean. Gungun and Arif have decided to plant some seeds but they do not know how to do it.

Let us find out how to plant seeds. Number the pictures correctly to help Gungun and Arif learn the right way of planting seeds.

6. Kuki Learns the Rules

Discuss

Look at the pictures. Talk about them in class.

Read along

Kuki goes to play in the park every evening.

Sometimes, she goes with her mother, and sometimes, with her father.

Today, Mother is with her.

As she reaches the park, she finds that a girl is already on the swing and another boy is waiting for his turn.

'I want to go first', says Kuki and stands in front of the boy.

'No, I am already in queue. You have to wait for your turn', says the boy.

Kuki is standing too close to the swing.

Mother says, 'Kuki, you must wait for your turn in the park and not stand too close to the swing. You may get hurt.'

Kuki then runs to the slide.

Here, she finds a queue too. She has an idea.

Instead of climbing the steps, she tries to climb up the slope of the slide. Of course, she slips down and falls on the grass with a bump.

Kuki starts crying.

Her mother says, 'Kuki, you should always climb up the stairs and slide down. The slope is not for climbing'.

'There are so many children', says Kuki. 'I will never get my turn'.

'Of course, you will', Mother says. 'If you follow the rules and be patient, everyone will get a turn to play.'

She says, 'I am sorry, Mother. From today onwards, I will wait for my turn in the park'.

'Good girl! This way, you will be safe too', her mother says with a smile.

Think and Say

Your friend is afraid of climbing monkey bars. How can you help her?

Remember

- Never go to the park alone.
- Wait for your turn at the swings.
- Do not talk to strangers at the park.
- Stand at a safe distance from the swings and other rides.
- Do not make the park dirty or pluck leaves and flowers.

Figure out

Tick (✓) the correct answers.

1. Kuki goes to the park with her mother or father because she is a
   a. small child.
   b. naughty child.
2. The boy waits for his turn because he is a
   a. lazy boy.
   b. responsible boy.
3. Kuki's mother asks Kuki to stand away from the swing because she may
   a. get hurt.
   b. climb on to it.
4. Kuki climbs the slide up the sloping side. This shows that she is
   a. a patient child.
   b. an impatient child.
5. Every child will get a turn on the swing if they
   a. fight for it.
   b. wait for it.

Relate

Draw a 🙂 for the best answer.

1. You are in the park eating a banana. Where where will you throw the peel?

a. On the ground

b. In the dustbin

2. You want to play on the swing but there is a long queue. What would you do?

a. Stand in queue and wait for my turn

b. Push other children to take my turn

3. You are playing cricket with your friends and other children want to join you. What would you do?

a. Refuse angrily

b. Let them play

Happiness Box

1. Red Rover, Red Rover

a. Form two groups and stand in two rows— Row A and Row B. Keep some space between the two rows for running.

b. In each row, hold hands tightly.

c. Call each student from the first row. For example, 'Red Rover, Red Rover, let Misha come over'.

d. The chosen student should run to Row B, trying to break through the clasped hands of the students in the first row.

e. If the student breaks through, he or she chooses someone from that Row B and takes the person back to Row A.

f. If the student is not able to break through then he or she joins Row A.

g. The game ends when all the students are in a single row.

2. Go to a lakeside or a forest with an elder. Collect different things from there like stones, pebbles, leaves, twigs and fruits. Bring them home and keep them in an box. Invite your friends and show them your treasure box.

Teaching tips

- Talk about good manners to be followed when the children are at a park.
- Give them some problematic situations and ask them what they would do in those situations.
- Tell them that parks are public places, so they belong to them too. Spoiling them means spoiling their own playing areas.

7. Lola's Drawings

Discuss

Look at the pictures. Talk about them in class.

Read along

Lola is six years old.

Everybody likes her as she is a neat girl.

When she comes back from school, she keeps her bag on the table and her shoes on the shoe rack. She also puts her uniform in the washing basket.

She loves reading and playing games. She also loves writing and drawing on the walls of her room.

Her mother does not like this. 'Lola, use your notebook to write and draw', she scolds Lola.

Lola doesn't listen to her mother.

Her father tried talking to her. He said, 'Lola, why do you spoil the beautiful walls of your room?'

Nothing changes Lola and she does not stop scribbling on the walls.

Then, one day, Lola's best friend Sally, comes to visit her.

Think and Say

You keep your room neat and clean but when your friends visit you, they make your room dirty. What would you do?

Lola wants to show Sally her wall drawings.

'Let us go and sit in my room', says Lola.

Sally does not like what she sees on the walls.

'Lola, your room is so neat and beautiful. What have you done to the walls?' she says.

'I often write or just draw on the walls. Do you think it is dirty!' says Lola. She then looks around her room and the walls.

'You are right, Sally. I have spoilt my neat and clean room. From today onwards, I will stop scribbling on the walls', says Lola.

Lola's parents heard her promise. They are happy that Lola has finally understood. Next day, Lola's parents stuck a big chart paper on the wall. Lola could scribble as much as she wanted without spoiling her room!

Remember

- It is our responsibility to clean our room.
- We should keep our room neat and clean.
- Keeping windows open lets fresh air come into the room.
- Keep things in their right places.

Figure out

Tick (✓) the correct answers.

1. Lola is a neat girl, so everyone

   a. likes her. ☐ b. dislikes her. ☐

2. Lola puts her things in the right places. She keeps her room

a. untidy. ☐ b. tidy. ☐

3. We should write or draw on

a. paper. ☐ b. walls. ☐

4. Lola's parents ask her to stop writing and drawing on the wall because it makes the room

a. dirty. ☐ b. beautiful. ☐

5. When Sally sees Lola's wall drawings, she

a. likes them very much. ☐ b. does not like them. ☐

Relate

Draw a 🙂 for the best answer.

1. It is raining and your shoes are dirty when you come back home. What would you do?

a. Enter the room with your dirty shoes ○

b. Take off your shoes at the door ○

2. You are going to be served dinner. Where would you eat your dinner?

a. At the dining table ○

b. On the bed ○

3. You want to let in fresh air into your room. What would you do?

a. Open the window

b. Keep the window closed

Happiness Box

1. Read this poem aloud in class.

A Clean Room

Shoes in the hall
Mud on the wall,
Toys on the stairs
Dirty socks on a chair,
My room needs a cure
That is for sure,
Now things sit at places right
Wow! What a nice sight.
A clean room is . . . you see
As it should always be.

2. Write the names of the things you keep in your cupboard.

3. Write three words that mean the same as ‘clean’. What is the opposite of clean?

....

....

....

....

Teaching tips

- Talk about clean people and how they are liked by everyone.
- Discuss how dirt can make you sick.
- Talk about dirty bathrooms and how to keep them clean after use. Many children believe it is not their responsibility to flush or wash the sink after use.

8. The Little Blue Engine

Discuss

Look at the pictures. Talk about them in class.

Read along

There was once a little blue engine that lived at an old railway track. Its job was to simply pull a few cars on and off the tracks. And that was what it did, every day. It loved doing this.

One bright sunny morning, as it was busy doing its rounds, it saw a long train standing on the old railway track.

The long train was requesting all the engines to take it over the hill. The train was so long that every engine refused to do so.

Just as the little blue engine stood staring at it, the long train turned to it. The train asked the little blue engine if it could help it go over the hill. The little blue engine looked at the slope of the hill and gulped.

'I think I can,' whispered the little engine.

Think and Say

Your friend and you are doing a project together. You have finished your part in the project. Your friend is having difficulty in completing hers. What would you do?

'What?' exclaimed the other engines together.

'I think I can', said the engine again. This time, it said louder than the first time.

The little blue engine then put itself in front of the train and started pulling with all its might. It pulled and pulled and pulled.

It puffed and puffed and puffed up the hill. 'I think I can. I think I can', said the engine all the way to the top of the hill!

In no time, the little blue engine had reached the top of the hill.

All the big engines looked at the little blue engine. They were surprised that the little blue engine had pulled the long train up the hill! Now, going down the hill was easier. It was fun too.

'I thought I could. I thought I could', said the little blue engine to itself all the way down.

The little engine believed it could do it. Therefore, it was able to do it.

– Adapted from the story The Little Engine that Thought it Could

Remember

- Being determined means never giving up and to keep on trying.
- We can do anything if we make up our mind for it.
- No task is impossible if we believe in ourselves.
- When you feel that it is difficult to do something, start telling to yourself, 'I think I can', just like the little blue engine.

Figure out

Tick (✓) the correct answers.

1. The little blue engine loved
   a. pulling cars on and off the tracks. ☐
   b. its colour. ☐

2. The big engines did not take the long train over the hill because
   a. they would have to work hard. ☐
   b. they were very naughty. ☐

3. The little blue engine agreed to take the long train over the hill because
   a. it wanted to test itself. ☐
   b. it wanted to help the long train. ☐

4. While going up the hill, the little blue engine kept saying to itself,
   a. I think I can ☐
   b. I thought I could ☐

5. The little blue engine was able to take the long train over the hill because
   a. it made up its mind to do it. ☐
   b. the larger engines had made fun of it. ☐

6. All the big engines were surprised because
   a. the little blue engine had broken down
   b. the little blue engine had pulled the long train up the hill

Relate

Draw a 🙂 for the best answer.

1. You are not able to learn dancing. What would you do?

a. Stop and start crying

b. Try till you learn it

2. Your friend is teaching you cartwheels. How would you learn to do them?

a. You would not learn how to do them

b. You would practise along with him

3. Your friend is sad as she did not get good marks in the class test. What would you do?

a. Tell her that she can do better in the next test

b. Give her a treat as you have scored well

Happiness Box

1. Say a story about how this boy overcame his fear and crossed the stream to meet his mother. Then color the picture using bright colors.

2. Look at these pictures. Tick the things you are determined to do.

I am determined to reach school on time. ◯

I am determined to win the game. ◯

I am determined to save electricity. ◯

I am determined to not waste paper. ◯

Teaching tips

- Talk about how strong determination helps the boy cross the stream.
- Tell children more stories about determination.

9. A Good Deed

Discuss

Look at the pictures. Talk about them in class.

Read along

It was Swati's birthday. All her friends came for the party that evening. The party had all of Swati's favourite things.

There were balloons and streamers hung across the room. The table was heaped with cupcakes, sandwiches, chips, chocolates, vegetable cutlets, patties, juices, sweets and candies of all kinds. There was a big, pink birthday cake.

The party was wonderful. The children enjoyed themselves. They played games, sang songs and danced till their feet hurt. They filled their plates again and again and ate happily.

But Swati's mother saw that a lot of food was left.

Think and Say

Sometimes, we cannot go out and celebrate birthdays or do the things we like to do. How would you celebrate your friends birthday if you cannot make it to her house party?'.

She called the children and said, 'Children, we should not waste food. Anybody who wants to eat more, please do so'. Some children took a cake slice or a cutlet, but still a lot of food was left.

Then Swati's mother called up someone to pick up food from her house. A van drove up to Swati's house. Mother gave the leftover food to the man in the van.

He said, 'Thank you Ma'am. I will give the food to poor children. They will be happy'.

Swati hugged her mother and said, 'Thank you, Mother!' Her friends also conveyed their thanks to her.

Remember

- Everyone needs food to grow.
- We must not waste food.
- Always offer food to someone who is hungry.
- We are lucky to have as much food as we need. Many people in this world do not get food to eat.

Figure out

Tick (✓) the correct answers.

1. The table was heaped with food as
   a. it was Swati's birthday. ☐
   b. Swati was very hungry. ☐
2. Swati's mother told the children to eat as much food as they could because
   a. she felt the children were hungry. ☐
   b. food must not be wasted. ☐
3. Swati's mother
   a. called someone to pick up the leftover food. ☐
   b. threw all the leftover food in the dustbin. ☐
4. The food that Swati's mother gave away was
   a. sent to some other party. ☐
   b. used to feed poor children. ☐
5. Swati's mother gave away all the leftover food
   a. so that food would not be wasted. ☐
   b. because there was no space in the house to keep the food. ☐

Relate

Draw a 🙂 for the best answer.

1. You see that your sister is unable to finish the food on her plate every day. What would you do?

a. Ask her to take only as much as she can eat ○

b. Let her waste food every day ○

2. You are unable to finish the rolls that you got in your lunch box. What would you do?

a. Throw them in the dustbin

b. Offer them to your friends

3. Your mother has made a new dish for you. What would you do?

a. Take a little bit, taste it and then decide if you want more

b. Fill your plate and if you do not like it, throw it

Happiness Box

1. Follow these steps to make a delicious fruit salad.

You need

- Sliced fruits
- Salt
- Lemon juice

a. Take the sliced fruits in a bowl.

b. Sprinkle some salt over them.

c. Pour lemon juice on the fruit pieces.

d. Toss the pieces to mix them.

e. Your delicious fruit salad is ready.

2. Learn this poem and sing it in class.

The Walrus and The Baker's Man

A loaf of bread, the Walrus said,
Is what we chiefly need:
Pepper and vinegar besides
Are very good indeed:
Now if you are ready, Oysters, dear,
We can begin to feed!

–Lewis Carroll

Teaching tips

- Stress on the fact that while students refuse to eat food that they do not like, many children do not have that choice.
- Tell the students how Gandhiji ate only one meal a day to understand the importance of food.

10. Minnie at School

Discuss

Look at the pictures. Talk about them in class.

Read along

Hello! My name is Minnie and this is my classroom.

The students in the class are my classmates.

There is a chair and a desk for every child. Our teacher sits on the big chair. She also has a big table. We greet her every day.

Our teacher writes on the blackboard. She checks our work. She loves us and we also love her a lot.

We keep our books in our desks. Sometimes, our teacher shares our drawings on the display board.

We always throw trash in the bin and keep the class neat and clean.

We do not talk when the teacher is teaching.

When I forget to take my pencil box, my classmates share their pencils and erasers with me.

Think and Say

Your teacher asks a question. Many students in your class start shouting the answer. Will you do the same? What would you do?

When the teacher asks us a question, we raise our hands and wait for our turn. We do not shout out the answers.

When we need to go out, we ask our teacher.

During lunch break, I share my lunch with my friends.

I love my class and my school.

Remember

- Take care of your classroom just as you take care of your home.
- Share responsibilities with your classmates.
- Help each other in class.
- Learn, share and have fun in your class.

Figure out

Tick (✓) the correct answers.

1. The teacher pins our drawings to the
   a. display board. ☐
   b. blackboard. ☐
2. While the teacher is teaching, we
   a. should talk. ☐
   b. should not talk. ☐
3. We can keep the classroom clean by using the
   a. broom. ☐
   b. dustbin. ☐

4. The students in the class are our
   a. classmates. ☐
   b. neighbours. ☐
5. If we need to go out of the class, we should
   a. ask the teacher first. ☐
   b. leave without asking the teacher. ☐

Relate

Draw a 🙂 for the best answer.

1. When the teacher comes into the class, what should we do?

a. Stand up and greet her ◯

b. Keep sitting ◯

2. Your classmate does not know the answer to a question. What would you do?

a. Laugh at your classmate ◯

b. Help your classmate after class ◯

3. When the teacher is not in the class, how should we behave?

a. Sit quietly ◯

b. Move around and make noise ◯

Happiness Box

1. **In your class, form groups of four. Each group gets a responsibility for a week. Interchange each group's work every day.**

Week 1	Group A	Check the nails of all students in class.
	Group B	Decorate the display board.
	Group C	Take care that all the students return to class on time, after lunch.
	Group D	Help the teacher.

2. **Make a list of things that you need to do to be ready for school the next day. Paste this list on your cupboard.**

Teaching tips

- Stress on self-discipline. Organising our lives helps us to reach our goals.
- Talk about how disciplined children are liked by everyone.
- Stress on discipline in public places, for example, inside a lift, in a movie hall and in a supermarket among others.

Goal 1: No Poverty

One in every ten people on Earth live in poverty. There are many who do not have work or homes and live on the streets.

Some of the things that people living in poverty cannot have are:

- Food
- Clean water
- Home
- Clothes and shoes
- Medicines
- Education

Let Us Think!

People most affected by poverty are:

- Workers
- Garbage collectors
- Helpers
- Vegetable sellers
- Porters
- Farmers

Take a Stand!

- Treat all people with with respect. Do not avoid them because of how they look.
- Clean out your closet. Give old books and toys to children from poor families.
- Do not waste food.
- Share your things and food with people who need them.

Project II : Look Out!

There are many things in our kitchen that can hurt us. How good are you at spotting things that can hurt us? Let us do an activity to find out.

Colour the picture of the untidy kitchen. There are ten things in there which can harm you. Spot and circle them.

If you have spotted:

- **6 things:** Go ahead, you can spot more.
- **7 things:** You have done a fair job, keep looking.
- **8 things:** Good going. Find the rest.
- **9 things:** Excellent, only one to go.
- **10 things:** Bravo, you are a genius.

Answers with reasons: Knife: You can cut yourself with this. Electric wire: Anyone can trip and fall down. Cockroach spray: If you breathe the spray, it can make you ill. Plastic bag: If you put it over your head, you will not be able to breathe. Unbalanced cup with hot tea: If the cup falls, it can burn you. Mop and water: You can slip in the water spill. Hot teapot: If you touch the hot teapot, it will hurt you. Stove: The flames from the stove can burn you. Even if the stove is not on, it might be hot. Touching it could burn your fingers. Open oven door: This will be hot and will hurt you while moving around. Standing on the stool: The stool can get unbalanced and you can fall.